This book belongs to

PREFACE

Welcome to a world of adventure and discovery brought to you by LightHouse Publications!

Each page of this book is a gateway to new ideas and exciting journeys that will inspire young minds to explore, learn, and grow. Our stories are lovingly crafted, combining vibrant illustrations by Sona with words that spark imagination and curiosity. Children are invited to travel to distant lands, solve curious puzzles, or meet fantastical creatures. With themes of bravery, kindness, and wonder, our books aim to instill a lifelong love of reading and discovery.

Dive into these pages and enjoy a magical journey that stretches the limits of the imagination and nurtures the spirit of adventure in every child.

MESSAGE TO THE PARENTS

Dear Parents,

Thank you for choosing a story from LightHouse Publications to share with your child. Our books are designed not just to entertain but also to educate and inspire. They encourage young readers to embrace kindness, courage, and curiosity about the world around them.

You'll notice a few challenging words included in the story. We've included these with the hope that you'll explain their meanings to your little ones. This not only helps in expanding their vocabulary but also enhances the precious time you spend reading together, strengthening your bond.

If you've enjoyed our story, please consider leaving an honest review on the storefront where you purchased this book. Your feedback is invaluable and helps us improve the quality of our books. Follow us on Instagram for more updates: @light.house_illustrations.

We believe that stories are a powerful tool for nurturing empathy, bravery, and wisdom in our children. So, cuddle up, turn the pages, and let's help them learn about the world in the coziest corner of your home.

With gratitude,
LightHouse Publications

IND

EX

WHAT ARE ALL THE BRIGHT OBJECTS IN THE SKY?

THE SKY IS LIKE A GIANT MYSTERY BOOK! LET'S DISCOVER ITS SECRETS!

WHEN YOU LOOK UP AT NIGHT, A BLANKET OF TWINKLING LIGHTS COVERS THE SKY.

Hi there! I'm Astro. Let's explore the amazing sky together!

THE SOLAR

The solar system, a family so grand,
With the Sun as the boss,
it takes command.
Planets, moons, and rocks take a ride,
In the vast, endless space
where wonders reside!

SYSTEM

The Sun's the center, the family's heart,
With planets as kids,
each playing their part.
They circle around in paths they hold,
A cosmic dance, a story told.

THE SUN

The Sun is a golden ball,
glowing warm and bright,
Shining down upon us,
spreading its light.

It's the heart of our system,
where planets align,
Dancing in circles, a cosmic design.

The Sun is so big, it's hard to decide—
But a million Earths could easily fit
inside!

A fiery sphere, with
gases so vast,
Hydrogen and helium in
a hot, bright mass.
It blazes with power, an
eternal flame,
The Sun, our star, by its
radiant name.

DID YOU KNOW?

Sunlight travels, fast and bright,
At the incredible speed of light.
From 93 million miles away,
It takes 8 minutes
to brighten our day!

THE PLANETS

Planets are big, round space balls,
Some are tiny, some are tall.
They're made of rock, gas, or ice,
Spinning around the Sun so nice!

MERCURY

Mercury is the
closest to the Sun,

Small and swift, its
race is never done.

VENUS

Venus shines with a
golden glow,
The hottest planet,
with clouds in tow.

Called the Morning
Star, it lights the skies,
A fiery world where
brightness lies.

EARTH

Earth is the planet we call home,

With oceans vast and lands to
roam.

MARS

Mars, the red planet,
dusty and dry,
Dreams of explorers
reaching its sky.

MARS

Mars has two moons,
a tiny pair,
Phobos and Deimos,
they're always there.

PHOBOS

MOONS

Orbiting close in the Martian sky,
Small and swift, they circle high!

DEIMOS

JUPITER

Jupiter is so massive, it's hard to comprehend its size—
Over 1,300 Earths could fit inside!.

The giant with
storms so grand,
Its Great Red Spot a
sight so planned.

JUPITER

Jupiter boasts 95 moons in its sky,
A satellite system where wonders lie
The Jovian system, a celestial delight,
With moons that shimmer in the night.

S MOONS

The Galilean four, so massive
and bright,
Lo, Europa, Ganymede, and
Callisto take flight.
A dance of giants,
a cosmic view,
In Jupiter's realm, where
dreams come true!

SATURN

Saturn with rings, a stunning view,
A cosmic jewel in the galaxy's blue.

So light, it could float in water
with ease—
If bathtubs were made for planets
like these!

SATURN'S
MOONS

It has 145 moons, both big and small,
From Titan to pebbles,
they orbit them all.
A circle of friends in a cosmic flow,
And scientists say the number may grow!

DID YOU KNOW?

Saturn's so light, it could float with ease,
In a tub big enough to span the seas.
And those rings? They stretch so wide—
73,000 kilometers from side to side!
That's like nine Earths in a cosmic row,
But they're thin as paper, as delicate as snow.
Amazing, isn't it, how fragile they seem?
Yet they sparkle in space, like a dream!

URANUS

Uranus spins with a tilted grace,
A pale blue orb,
in the vastness of space.

Freezing cold, with a frosty hue,
Its faint, icy rings are a stunning view.

URANUS'
MOONS

It has 27 moons, a celestial team,
With names from poems and
Shakespeare's dream.
Titania, Oberon, Miranda—so bright,
Each adds magic to the cosmic night.

DID YOU KNOW?

Uranus spins in a frozen place,
A short 17 hours for its daily race.
But its year takes 84 Earthly rounds,
In its distant orbit, where mystery abounds!

NEPTUNE

Neptune's winds are the fastest known,
A world of storms where mysteries are sown.

The farthest from the Sun,
A journey so long, it's never done.
One orbit takes 165 years,
Through icy depths and frozen spheres!

NEPTUNE'S
MOONS

Neptune, with moons that number
fourteen,
In the icy depths, a stunning scene.
Triton, the largest, leads the crew,
Orbiting backward—how cool and true!

DID ✦ YOU KNOW?

Neptune's winds are the fastest around,
Faster than sound, they fiercely pound.
At 1,200 miles per hour they race,
A wild, windy party in cosmic space!

PLUTO

Pluto, so small, an icy delight,
Lives in the Kuiper Belt, far from sight.
A tiny world in a distant place,
A frozen gem in the vastness of space!

Once called a planet with pride, Now a dwarf planet, where mysteries hide.

PLUTO'S
MOONS

Pluto has five moons in its icy domain,
Charon, the largest, leads the chain.
So big, it dances with Pluto, a pair,
Spinning together in cosmic flair.
Styx, Nix, Kerberos, Hydra join in,
Tiny companions in a celestial spin.
Out in the Kuiper Belt, far and bright,
Pluto's a marvel, a distant delight!

48

DID YOU KNOW?

Pluto has a heart, so icy and bright,
A giant wonder in the cosmic night.
It's bigger than countries, a frozen mark,
Guiding its spin through the endless dark.

THE MOON

"NIGHT'S SHINING FRIEND"

When the day ends and darkness falls,
The Moon smiles down on us all.
A gentle glow, so calm and bright,
Guiding dreams through the quiet night.

The Moon goes round Earth in a steady run,
Just like we circle around the Sun.
A cosmic dance, both near and far,
Guided by gravity, our shining star.

MOON'S PHASES

Sometimes the Moon is full
and bright,
Lighting up the quiet night.
Other times, it's a tiny slice,
A silver glow that still feels nice.

"
Astronauts have
walked on the Moon

Would you like to visit
the Moon someday?
"

The first to walk on the Moon so wide,
Was Neil Armstrong, with fearless stride.
A giant leap for all mankind,
A moment in history, one of a kind.
And Valentina, brave and bold,
Flew to space, a story told.
The first woman to soar so high,
Touching the stars in the endless sky!

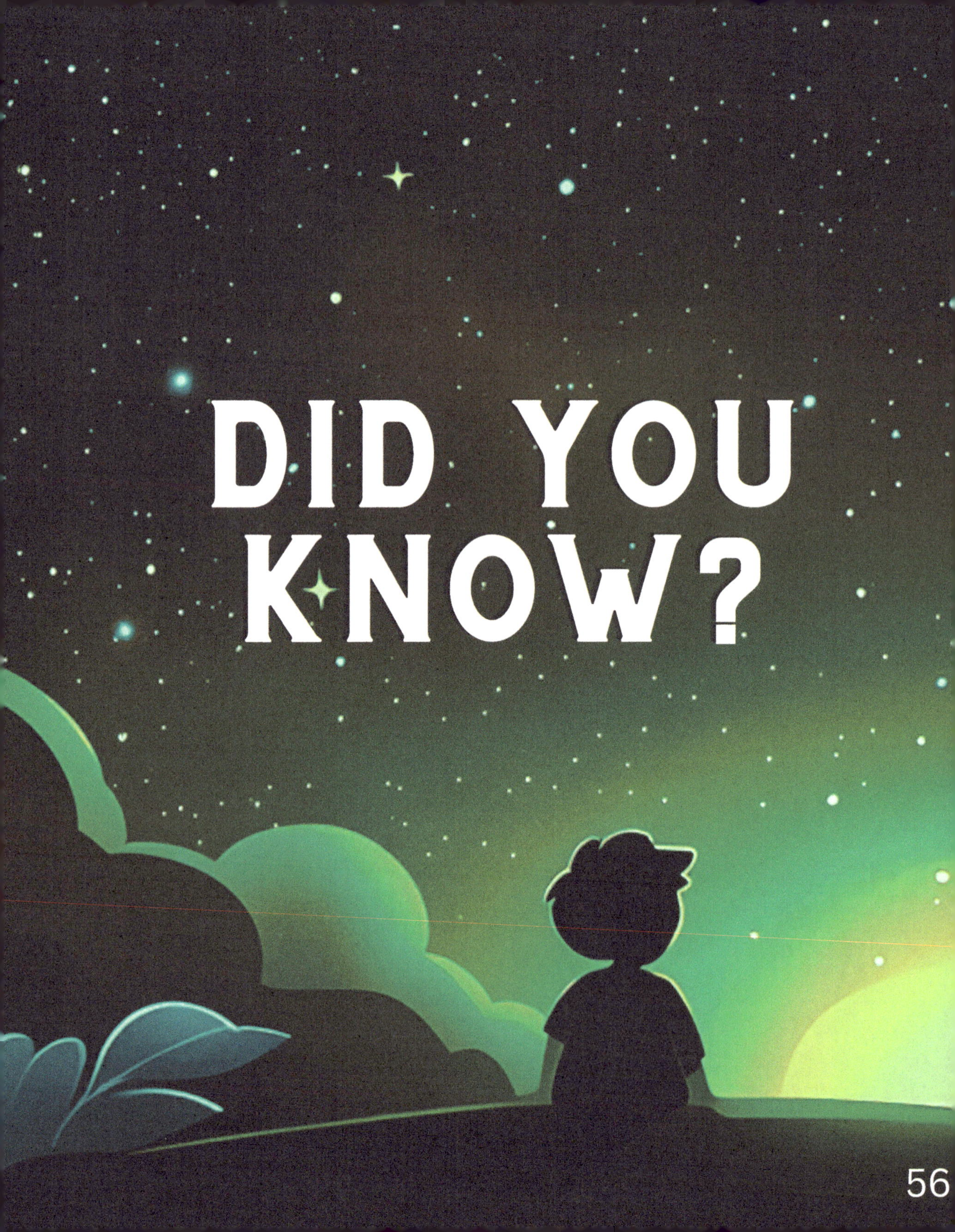
DID YOU
KNOW?

Moonlight isn't its own bright gleam,
It's sunlight reflected, a shining beam.
The Moon takes the Sun's glow and shares it with care,
Lighting the night with a sparkle so rare.
So when you see the Moon shining so high,
It's sunlight bouncing in the sky.
A gentle glow, borrowed light,
Guiding us softly through the night.

THE TWINKLING STARS

Stars are tiny, twinkling lights,
Sprinkled across the sky at night.
Faraway Suns, they shimmer and glow,
Lighting the darkness with a cosmic show.

TYPES OF STARS

There are different colors of stars

Coolest stars

Hottest stars

Yellow Stars are like our Sun

Mix of both hot and cool

SHOOTING STARS

This is a shooting star, so bright,
A tiny spark in the dark of night.
It zooms across the sky so fast,
A fleeting moment that doesn't last.
Make a wish as it streaks on through,
A magical sight for me and you!

DID YOU KNOW?

A shooting star, not a star at all,
But a tiny rock that takes a fall.
It burns so bright as it streaks
through air,
A fiery show, a moment rare.

CONSTELLATIONS: PICTURES IN THE SKY

A constellation is a starry delight,

A picture drawn in the sky at night.

Like a bear, a hunter,

or a crown so high,

Stories are told where the stars lie.

62

ANIMAL CONSTELLATION

Some constellations, bright and grand,
Look like animals across the land.
Ursa Major, the Great Big Bear,
Roams the night sky, always there.
Canis Major, the loyal hound,
Follows the hunter, stars abound.

SHAPE CONSTELLATIONS

Some stars make shapes in the sky so high,
Like a big spoon called Ursa Major nearby.
And look for a W, shining with glee,
That's Queen Cassiopeia for all to see.

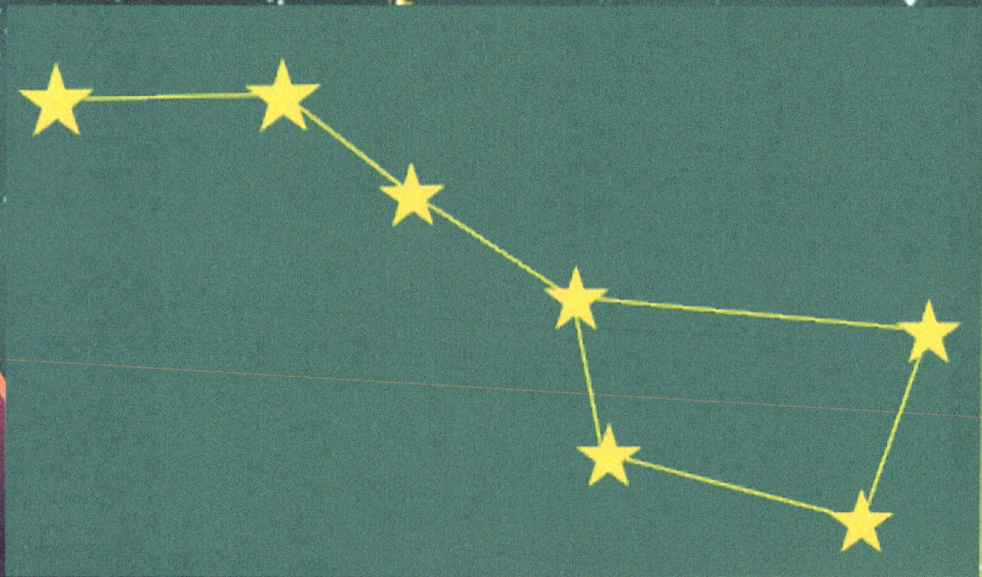

PEOPLE CONSTELLATIONS

Some constellations take human form,
Like Orion, the Hunter,
through the night he storms.
With his bow and belt, he lights the sky,
A timeless figure, standing high.

DID YOU KNOW?

Constellations change as the seasons go,
New ones appear with a celestial show.
Winter's Orion, with stars so bright,
And summer brings the Swan in flight.

As Earth orbits, the patterns shift,
A starry treasure, a seasonal gift.
Look to the skies, and you will see,
A changing map of astronomy!

SPACE ROCKS

ASTEROIDS AND COMETS

"Rocks and ice sail through space,

tiny travelers in a race."

Watch out for space rocks

COMETS

Comets streak with a glowing tail,
Icy wanderers, they leave a trail.
Born in the Kuiper Belt's frozen embrace,
They journey far through endless space.

Comet

ASTEROIDS

Asteroid Belt

Asteroids roam in the vast dark sea,
Rocks in space, wild and free.
Some are tiny, some are grand,
Leftover pieces of the solar band.

70

ASTEROID BELT

The asteroid belt, a rocky line,
Between Mars and Jupiter, it does shine.
A path of stones, both big and small,
A cosmic border, a space-rock wall.

Asteroid Belt

Jupiter

Mars

GALAXIES

Galaxies are cosmic towns,
Full of stars that swirl around.
Billions shining, near and far,
Each a cluster, a stellar bazaar.

Some are spirals with arms that spin,
Others are round, a glowing grin.
From dwarfs to giants, they light the night,
Galaxies are wonders, a breathtaking sight.

THE MIL

Our Starry

Our galaxy is Milky Way, with stars so many, bright and gay.

We live in the Milky Way galaxy!

KY WAY

ome

It's like a giant city of stars!
Our solar system is just a tiny part.

NEIGHBOR GALAXIES

OUR STARRY HOME

Beyond our galaxy so wide, other starry homes reside.

Neighbor galaxies,
close to our own,
In the vast universe,
they're brightly shown.

Let's visit other galaxies!

The Milky Way's friends
in the cosmic sea,
Andromeda and Triangulum,
shining with glee.

ANDROME

Andromeda shines in the sky so wide,
A spiral galaxy by our side.

DA GALAXY

Our closest neighbor, vast and bright,
A cosmic gem in the endless night.

TRIANGUL

Triangulum, a galaxy small,
Yet its beauty can captivate all.

UM GALAXY

It looks like a spiral, just like the Milky Way, and it's really, really far—about 3 million light-years away!

ASTRONAUTS
JOURNEY INTO SPACE

Up, up, up the rocket go, carrying astronaut you know.

HOW ROCKETS WORK

A rocket goes up with a big bright flame, flying to space like it's playing a game!

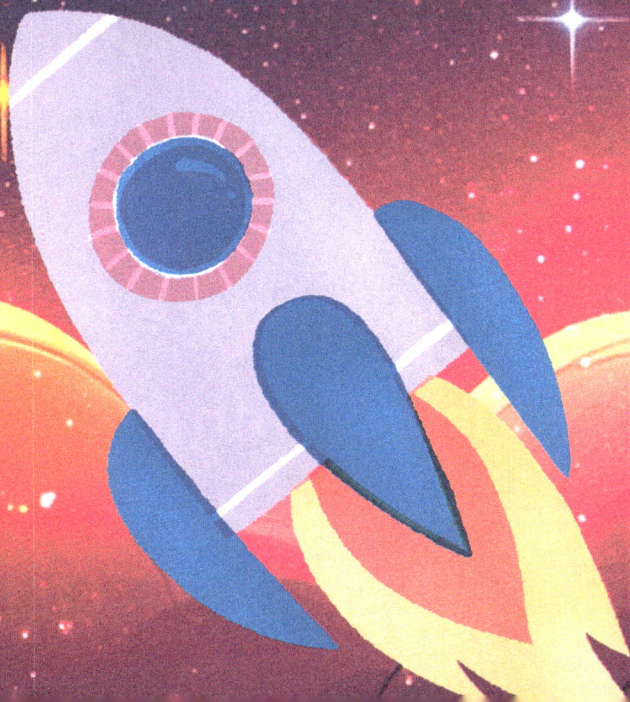

DID YOU KNOW PEOPLE LIVE IN SPACE?

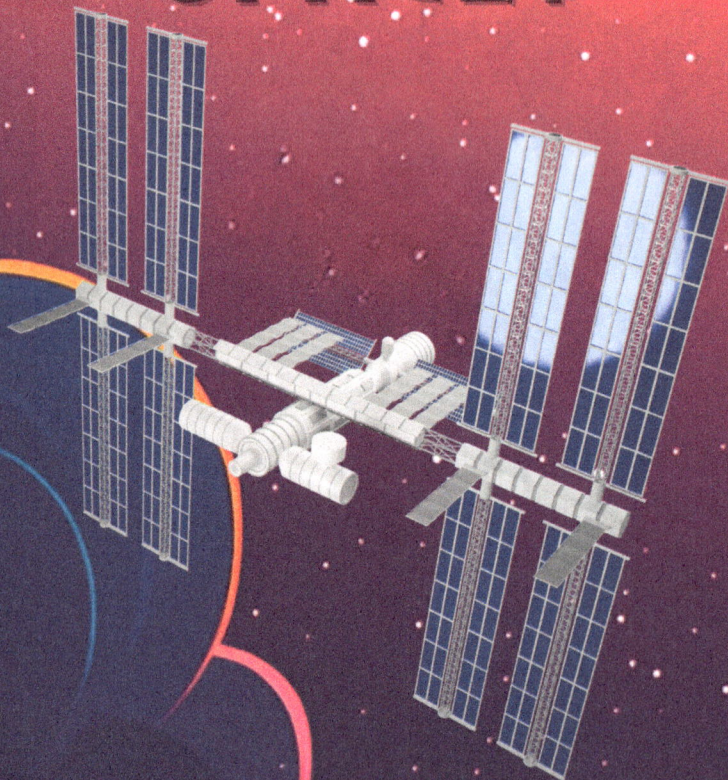

Astronauts live in space for a while,
To work and learn with a curious smile.
They study stars and planets so far,
Exploring the secrets of each shining star.

84

Floating in space, they boldly go,
In the vast unknown,
where wonders glow.
A little while, but their mission's grand,
Expanding our knowledge,
hand in hand!

WHAT DO YOU HAVE TO STUDY TO BE AN ASTRONAUT?

To be an astronaut, you need to prepare,
Learning of space and the stars out there.
How rockets soar and engines hum,
How to stay strong in the weightless realm

It's training for an adventure so high,
A journey beyond, up into the sky.
With knowledge and courage, you'll boldly explore,
A cosmic quest forevermore!

"WONDERS OF THE UNIVERSE"

NEBULAS

Nebulas

Stars are born in nebulas!

Nebulas are cosmic art, clouds of dust and stars apart.

DID YOU KNOW?

Nebulas are clouds, so colorful and wide,
A nursery for stars, where they come to abide.
Like the Orion Nebula, glowing so bright,
A masterpiece painted in the cosmic night.

"WONDERS OF THE UNIVERSE"
BLACK HOLES

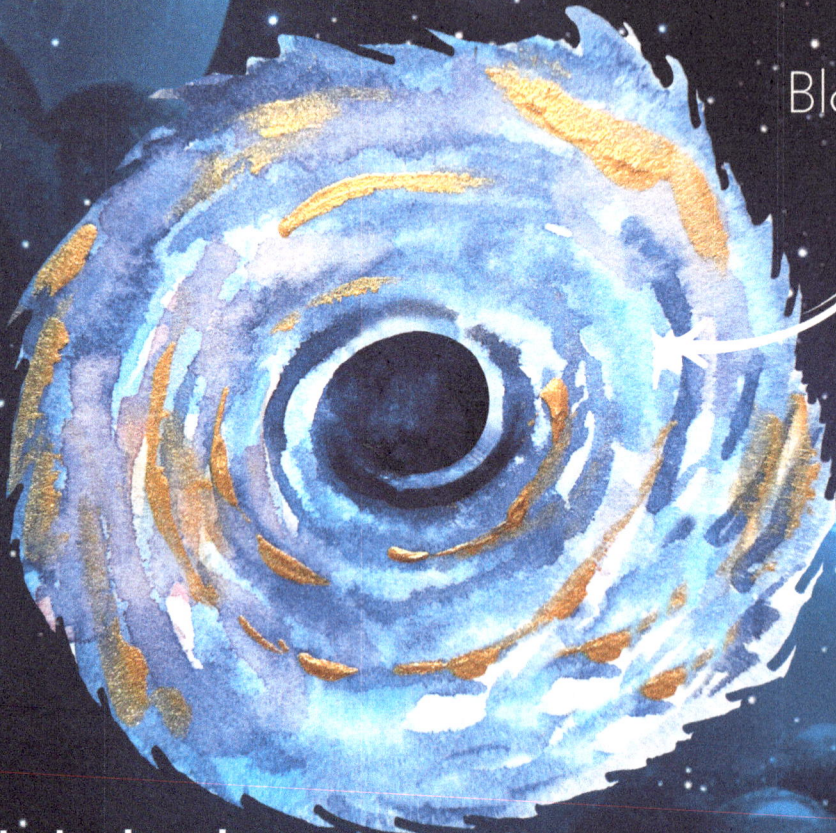

Black Hole

Black holes have super strong gravity
Black holes are mighty, dark, and grand,
With gravity's power, they rule the land.

90

DID YOU KNOW?

Black holes are strong, with a mighty pull,
So fierce they can swallow light whole.
But after a feast of gas and dust,
They "burp" out energy in a fiery thrust.

THE ENDLESS SKY AND YOU

The universe is vast and grand, bigger than we all can understand!

If Earth is a tiny dot, the universe is like a giant ocean!

Stretch your arms wide—

—that's how big space feels!

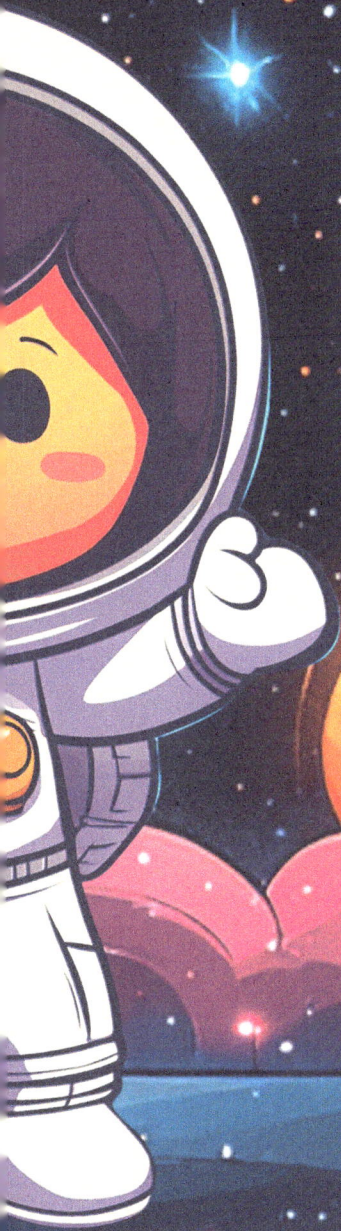

THE UNIVERSE IS YOURS TO EXPLORE, WITH COUNTLESS WONDERS TO ADORE

SEE YOU AMONG THE STARS!

Thank you for joining us on this delightful journey!

If you loved this story, don't forget to scan the QR code below to discover more wonderful books from LightHouse Publications and our sister publication, LightsOut Coloring. LightHouse Publications creates enchanting coloring books for both kids and adults, perfect for fostering creativity and relaxation. Explore our world of stories and coloring adventures today!

We're excited to bring more magical experiences into your home. Happy reading.